The Harvey Mackay Rolodex® Network Builder

by

Harvey B. Mackay

Published by Mackay Envelope Corporation
2100 Elm Street Southeast
Minneapolis, MN 55414
Manufactured in the United States of America

Includes Table of Contents
ISBN 0-9637967-0-4
®Rolodex is a registered trademark of Rolodex Corporation

Dedication

This book is dedicated to anyone who ever struggled—to find a job, buy a house, raise a child, start a business, finish school, make a sale, invent a product, get ahead, or make something happen.

Struggling is not a comfortable thing. It involves long hours of work, worry and wondering. Sometimes we achieve what we hoped to achieve, sometimes we don't. Often, the outcome is very different from what we had planned.

Luckily, there are some benefits to struggling. First, it helps us grow. Human beings tend to do their best work when they are overcoming the odds.

Second, we don't have to do it alone.

Wherever we're going, we all need the help of others to get there. Don't ever be afraid to ask for what you need. That's what your network is for. That's what your Rolodex file is for. There are plenty of people out there waiting and willing to help. All they ask is that some day, some time, some place, you find a way to pass it on.

Harvey Mackay

Preface

There we sat, in a crowded stadium watching a heated match at the U.S. Open Tennis Tournament, and Carol Ann was talking.

Twenty thousand people and I were there to concentrate. Carol Ann, it seems, was there to network—a skill she has raised to an art over the years. And, when you think about it, what better place to meet interesting people than the U.S. Open with its boisterous New York crowd and combustible atmosphere?

However, that day I was in the mood for tennis. I tried a few pointed glances and then a loud "shhhhh." These were blithely ignored.

By then I was so distracted I missed the winning point and the match ended. Carol Ann turned to me, beamed and announced: "That was the best point of the match." Then she went back to talking with her new-found friend.

Eavesdropping, I got the gist of their conversation. Carol Ann had informed her that while we were in New York, we were visiting our daughter, Mimi, who had recently moved there with an advertising degree to try to crack the job market. It seems this woman had played college tennis and now worked for a prominent Madison Avenue ad agency. She was giving Carol Ann all sorts of tips about which firms were good places to work and which were sweat shops, who to talk to, what they looked for in applicants—invaluable information only someone in the know could have possibly provided. In fact, she subsequently invited Mimi, who had also played college tennis, to interview with her firm.

Not longer after that visit, Mimi was hired by the same agency. It's a great example of what I firmly believe about networking: To be truly successful in life and in business, you have to have a genuine curiosity about people and a real willingness to work at keeping relationships going over time. That's both a gift and a skill. I can't help you much with the gift part—you either like people or you don't. But I can help you master the skills. Remember, no matter how good you are, you're really only as good as the network you build. Now, let's get started. . .

Acknowledgments

I would like to gratefully acknowledge Lynne Lancaster for her help in putting this guide together. Her marketing know-how, insight, and true professionalism have been invaluable.

Also, thanks to my sister, Margie Mackay Resnick, for being my personal editor on all my projects.

Table of Contents

Lesson 1

It's A Chronicle
Of Your Life.

One of the most important words in the English language isn't in the dictionary. It's Rolodex[1]. And I wouldn't be a bestselling author or successful businessman today without it. What does Rolodex, a routine filing system for phone numbers, have to do with literary success? Let me tell you how it changed my life.

Every year, over 600,000 manuscripts make their way to publishers. Of these, about 55,000 get printed, only a handful make it onto the *New York Times* Best Seller List, and just a couple make it to Number One.

Because the odds are so great against any one book hitting it big, publishers are extremely cautious about the number of books they print in the first edition of a new book. That goes double for business books, and probably triple for first-time unknown authors from the fly-over state of Minnesota. Even though the first printing of a book is critical, publishers will typically print only about 10,000 copies. That way, if the book doesn't

[1]Rolodex is a registered trademark of Insilco Corporation

make it, the company can more easily cover its losses.

The irony is that, as I quickly learned, the single biggest factor in undermining a new book's success is the lack of them in bookstores. If the books aren't in the stores, people can't buy them. The first printing is vital for another reason, too. If the publisher makes a big commitment to the author up front, they are much more likely to spend the time and money needed to promote the book.

An old friend and successful author, Ken Blanchard, introduced me to William Morrow and Company. I sent Morrow a copy of my manuscript in advance, then started doing my homework to see if I couldn't increase my chances of hitting a 400 foot home run my first time at bat. Using my Rolodex card file, I called people all over the country who had any connection whatsoever with publishing. I called printers, editors, agents, lawyers, writers, journalists and owners of publishing companies. From my contacts, I learned the peculiarities of the publishing market...who to talk to, how to negotiate, what to ask for, when to ask for it, what was the market like, virtually every question I could think of.

Based on the information I accumulated, I made a plan. Then came time for my meeting with the Morrow people. I walked into the room and there sat the Chief Executive Officer, the President and the Senior Vice President—three grizzlies meeting an amateur. They had already seen my manuscript and were open to discussion, so things started out on a fairly pleasant note. The congenial mood in the room lasted just until I mentioned that I wanted them to seriously consider a first printing of my book of 100,000 copies. End of meeting. Basically, we were on the 16th floor and they invited me to jump. The silence was deafening. They started rustling their papers, closing their books, and checking their watches.

Finally, the Senior Sales Manager spoke up, "Well, obviously we're not going to have a chance to get together on this, but tell me, Mr. Mackay, who are you to come into this room and ask for a 100,000 hardcover first printing when most of the top books for the past forty years started out with about 10,000 copies? You're an unknown first-time author. We don't understand it."

I reached down under the table, opened my mini-suitcase and took out my Rolodex file. There sat the results of forty years of disciplined work: six thousand five hundred names. I started going through them. Some countries: France, England, Germany, Israel. Some companies: Pillsbury, General Mills, IBM. "Here's Honeywell", I said, "with 64,000 employees. Here's 3M with 85,000. I know quite a few people in those companies. And I think that if a couple of people buy the book they'll read it and pass it around."

On I went, through some of the movers and shakers I'd met over a lifetime of keeping my Rolodex file, pointing out those that I thought would be good candidates to ask for endorsements.

Three weeks and three meetings later, they agreed to print an unprecedented 100,000 hardcover books!

For me, that was the culmination of a forty-year journey. Like your record shelf or your book shelf, your Rolodex file is a chronicle of your life. It tells you where you've been, but unlike other monuments to the past, it can also tell you where you're going. There's almost no direction you can take in business, no decision you can make, that isn't already foreshadowed in your Rolodex file.

One of my favorite sayings is that you must dig your well before you're thirsty. During the years we spend meeting new people, following up with them, tracking their lives, we're really digging a well so that at some time in the future we can quench our thirst— for knowledge, contacts, ideas, assistance, information, whatever we need, whenever we need it.

THE ROLODEX NETWORK BUILDER

It's no surprise that my Rolodex file was the key to getting my book *published*, because in reality it was the key to getting it *written* in the first place.

When I started writing, I knew I couldn't write a collection of high-brow theories about business. What I wanted to write about was literally *in* my Rolodex file—a lifetime of stories and anecdotes and lessons learned from the people I've known over the years. There's no way you can glance at a Rolodex card without remembering the story behind the person.

People tend to think it's just names and addresses that make the Rolodex file work. They're wrong. The key to this system is having the strengths, weaknesses, interests, family background, hobbies and accomplishments of these people, all at your fingertips. You build that knowledge throughout a lifetime, and I've included my unique system in this book for you to start using right away.

No one on Earth can tell me where he's going to be ten years from now. You never know, that fellow student from drama class could become your biggest customer or the banker you need to help finance your new business. Several years ago, who would have guessed that jailed playwright Vaclav Havel would become President of Czechoslovakia?

The majority of students graduating from college today don't have the slightest idea what they want to do with their lives. To complicate matters, research tells us that today's college graduates will experience 10.3 job changes in his or her lifetime!

Your Rolodex file is a great way to survive those changes. Whether you're an entrepreneur, in sales, or aiming for another rung on the corporate ladder, you can reach out and tell the whole world about it. You can send out a laser-sharp mailing list, you can personalize it, and you can derive a lifetime of confidence knowing that all those people are keeping track of you and your progress.

As a parent, one of the best things I ever did for my kids, and one of the few decisions I've never second-guessed, was to get them started keeping a Rolodex file early in life. All three are in their 20's now, and I'd estimate they each have at least 500 names on file. In fact, my son David is close to hitting the thousand mark. The discipline and focus that might have seemed awkward at first has become a lifetime habit, and the contacts they've made give them a super leg-up on the competition.

My youngest daughter, Jojo, graduated as a dance major from the University of Michigan in the Spring of 1990. She knew she wanted to work in the field of dance, so she moved to New York City and started pounding the pavement. In her Rolodex file, she came across the name of someone whose kids she had met six years earlier on a a family vacation. She'd been in touch with them a few times over the years, and knew that the father now worked as a producer in New York. She called and reintroduced herself and he offered her several names of people she might talk to. Within a few weeks, she had a job teaching dance to children at a well-known and much respected private school.

If you're wondering about your own network building skills, take the self-quiz in Appendix I to see how you rate.

A fellow by the name of Elliott Jaques is the director of the Institute of Organization and Social Studies at Brunel University in England. He's made a career out of studying how executives think (that's *how* they think, not *whether* they think).

One of Jacques' key discoveries is what he calls the "time-frame of the individual." While some people find it difficult to plan out what they are going to do today or this week, others function comfortably within time-frames of several months to a year. His work with highly successful executives show they are able to shape plans that extend far into the future. Some Japanese executives, most notably the late President of Matsushita, can actually conceive of a two-hundred-year corporate plan!

In my opinion, the biggest constant over the lifetime of a career is the relationships we form. Although I have trouble envisioning exactly what my business will be like ten years from now, I know that whatever I'm doing will be based on the contacts I've already made and those I'm making today. In that way, my Rolodex file serves as a touchstone. It extends my personal time-frame far beyond what my brain could remember. It allows me to keep track of literally hundreds of people who, at some time or another, may become an active part of my life.

There's a great story about the high school baseball coach welcoming his players back in the Fall. They'd won two games and lost twenty-one the year before. He says, "I've got good news and bad news. The good news is, you're all back. The bad news? You're all back."

None of us can tell which contacts will be the most interesting or valuable to us as time passes. But with persistence and a genuine desire to stay close to the people we meet, we can expand our relationship time-frame to last a lifetime.

Lesson 2

Guard It With Your Life.

If I were being mugged and had to choose whether to hand over my wallet or my Rolodex file, it would be no contest. Losing a wallet is inconvenient, scary, expensive, and a pain in the back pocket. But losing my Rolodex file would be devastating. I can replace all my credit cards and I can live without a few dollars. But the information I've gathered over the years—now that's irreplaceable.

How do you do it? Like many great ideas, it's very simple. When you meet someone new, make note of when, where and how you met and anything interesting you learned about that person...hobbies, family data, special interests, etc. As soon as you get back to your office (and by this I mean *the same day*), make a Rolodex card and file it immediately. You should also note any follow-up contact—a thank you letter, an article sent out, whatever—and when your next contact will occur. That way you can make sure your Rolodex file is working actively for you, not just sitting dormant on your desk.

If you don't have a specific reason to contact

---

someone, you might still make a note to follow up in, say, six months. Later, when you get that reminder, you'll find a reason to be in touch. If you have a genuine desire to stay in contact, it's easy. Here are some examples:

You've changed jobs and you want to let people know where they can find you. You might send a formal announcement or a handwritten note with your new business card. You might also want to send a brochure that will interest them, or your new company's annual report.

A friend of mine makes a point of clipping and sending me ideas I can use in speeches. It might be a great quote, a funny story, or even a cartoon like the one I received in which a bumper sticker on a Texas car proclaimed, "Buy a toaster and get an S&L free!"

I'm always grateful for ways to add zing to my talks but I'm even more grateful to know someone's thinking about me.

Regardless of what you send, the message is clear: "I value your friendship and I want to stay in touch."

Meeting new people and developing your network doesn't mean much unless you creatively and painstakingly keep the relationship going over time.

It's like the meticulous spender. Everywhere

he went he carried a little black notebook where he recorded every single penny he ever spent—tips, parking fees, pay phones…you name it, he wrote it down. He only had one problem. He never stopped to add it up.

The key to building a network is keeping track of the small, seemingly insignificant details. As I discussed in my book, *Swim With The Sharks Without Being Eaten Alive*, little things don't mean a lot, they mean everything.

World class cyclist Greg LeMond is a super example. In the 1989 Tour de France, LeMond entered the final stage of the race trailing the leader by fifty seconds. He estimated that by riding the very best ride of his life he could make up about thirty seconds on the final leg—but that would still leave him twenty seconds behind overall. Somehow, somewhere, he would have to cut an additional twenty seconds off his time.

Sports Illustrated reported that as he raced through the final sprint, LeMond kept his head down and held perfect aerodynamic position, ignoring the screaming Americans crowding the sidelines and looking up only enough to keep himself on course.

He also wore a special aerodynamically-designed helmet to cut down on wind resistance against his head. For some unknown reason, his opponent, Laurent Fignon of France, chose to race the final leg without a helmet, pony tail streaming out behind him.

You wouldn't think a small thing like a helmet would make much difference in a road race that takes 23 days to complete and covers 2,025 miles.

The result says it all. Greg LeMond won the Tour de France by a margin of *eight seconds*!

That kind of success doesn't happen by accident. You can't turn it off and on like a light switch. It has to be a permanent part of your lifestyle. And your Rolodex file has to be used the same way. Once you start having fun with it, your antennae will always be up looking for new ways to use it. Using it becomes a way of life.

An old friend phoned me to tell me about his trip—he just returned from Siberia. Another day, Notre Dame football coach Lou Holtz called to tell me had just jumped out of an airplane. After conversations like these, I go to the Rolodex file and make a note: "Siberia, February 1990," or "Airplane jump, Spring 1990." I might not talk to that person again for months, but when I do you can bet I'll ask, "How's your skydiving?" or whatever.

Remember, pale ink is better than the most retentive memory. Once you write it down and you know where you can find it again, believe me, you're on your way.

Lesson 3

Consider It An Investment.

Throughout your whole life you build a network of people who reflect your values, your beliefs, what you stand for. Think of the hours you spend each day, each week, each month, each year, getting to know people. For some people, making personal contacts requires more time than any other activity in their weekly schedule. I know I spend at least thirty hours a week with customers, vendors, associates, friends and, of course, prospects.

Multiply that by fifty-two weeks and you're talking about a yearly total of more than *fifteen hundred hours* invested in getting to know people.

What becomes of that fifteen-hundred-hour investment if I don't follow through? If I don't write it all down and put it somewhere safe, how can I be absolutely 100% sure I won't forget about it? The answer is simple. That investment is down the drain unless I have way to organize it and make use of it. The only sure-fire way I've ever found is my Rolodex file.

Nowhere is the ability to develop a network more vital than in Hollywood. A recent *Newsweek*

21

article described how one firm, Triad Artists Agency, uses networking and the Hollywood grapevine to create a frenzy of interest over a new script just before they put it up for auction.

"As scripts come in, the agents rev up 'the buzz machine,' putting the word out. . .that a hot commodity will soon be on the block. If the buzz is loud enough, development execs and producers scramble over one another to get the first look. . . .Eventually, the buzz trickles to the top of the studios. . . .The game used to take days—now it can be over in a matter of hours."

Ok, so you're not a Hollywood mogul. What if you only do a little networking each week? The answer is: That's fine—as long as you know how to organize your results so they work for you.

Imagine you're a college student working a summer internship or spending Spring Semester doing informational interviewing (which is a super idea, by the way). Every day you meet new people. If you meet just two new people a week, that's one hundred and four people by the end of the year.

And that's just the beginning. Before you know it, your Rolodex file will begin to swell with names of people who know you, remember you, and are interested in seeing the direction your career takes.

In 1990, the Minnesota North Stars hockey team was in danger of being moved to California. I became part of a group determined to prove to the National Hockey League that we were willing to buy the team if necessary to keep it from leaving Minnesota. We had to raise $30 million in a matter of weeks, and the single tool that enabled us to do it was the Rolodex file.

We started calling people locally and around the country who we knew from the Rolodex file had some interest in hockey. One person was a former owner of an NHL team. A couple others were long-time hockey fans with connections to families who owned teams. Ultimately, we were able to demonstrate to the League we could organize a bona fide group of local buyers. The outcome was that the North Stars were sold, but they remained in the Twin Cities.

When you're building a network, it isn't important whether you start out big or small. You just have to do it right. Remember, we all start out in life with one thing in common. . .we all have the same amount of time. It's just a matter of what we do with it.

Lesson 4

Remembering Doesn't Work.

If you're young, you may have to take my word for it.

The fact is, it's embarrassing to be unable to recall a detail about someone you haven't seen for awhile. Most of us can barely retain the birthdays and anniversaries of our closest friends, let alone information about all the people who enter our business lives along the way. Some of us are hard-pressed to remember people's names without hoping to recall where they gave that great speech or what volunteer activities they're most proud of. Once you know more than twenty or fifty or a hundred people, it's hopeless. Unless you have a system.

Some of the most interesting research on the topic of memory deals with how we use visual cues to remember things. All of us have had the experience of sitting in a final exam unable to recall the answer to the question, but able to picture its exact location on the page in our textbook.

With the right visual cues, our memories are better than we think. Test yourself. Off the top of your head, how many people can you name from your high school graduating class? If you had enough time, I'll bet you could remember a couple dozen. But how many could you recall, in detail, if you had a visual cue—let's say you glanced through your yearbook? Of course you could remember many more, and it wouldn't be just names, faces and ridiculous haircuts. You'd suddenly have access to an amazing mental file of conversations, shared interests, embarrassing moments, and all the other little things relationships are made of.

Tests made on the brain suggest that we never really forget anything, we just misplace it somehow in that incredible computer that is the human mind. Most of our organizational systems are simply cues to the brain asking it to respond appropriately. Some are physical cues—like the stacks of papers I throw on the floor in front of my office door to remind me what to take home at night.

Others, like the Rolodex card file, are verbal and visual cues. When I look at a Rolodex card file, I immediately recall much more than what it says in a few lines. I know a whole person, and it's usually someone I'd like to know even better.

I've heard people complain that it's too much work, or that it's somehow artificial to keep notes on people you meet. My response is that for me it's not work, it's fun. And even if it takes a little effort, it's a lot less effort than it would take to replace that information later. There's nothing artificial about using cues to jog your memory.

The benefit of making a few notes on things that interest me about people is that when I meet them again, we can pick up where we left off. You can get to know people so much better if you don't have to begin each conversation with "Where do you work again?" or "Did you tell me you have children?" or "Aren't you involved with the Republican gubernatorial campaign, or was it the Democrats?"

I prefer to start off by saying, "How's it going at Acme Corporation? I read you acquired a widget manufacturing subsidiary. Aren't widgets a specialty of yours?"

It all stems from a very old principle. That is, treating others the way you'd like to be treated yourself. I know how great I feel when I run into somebody who remembers that my daughter and I run marathons together. Believe me, I'd much rather talk about that than the Dow Jones averages or the weather.

Conrad Hilton, founder of the multi-billion dollar hotel empire, was a master at treating people well—and at learning from his mistakes. In his book, *Be My Guest*, he recounts that early in his career, he bought his mother a diamond necklace with profits from one of his first hotel deals. It was an expensive and showy piece, far too elaborate for a lady of her age and elegant taste. Upon receiving it, she burst into tears and left the room. Later she acknowledged it was a wonderful gift but too "outstanding" for her to actually *wear*.

Hilton goes on to explain: "From that time on I began collecting and storing away little preferences that would make me a better gift giver, both personally and professionally...I know that when the late and wondrous Gertrude Lawrence was a guest at our Los Angeles hotel some years later, I was tickled that I had overheard her at a theatrical party tell a friend that the tiny white roses in her corsage were her favorite flower. And that gift, [of the corsage] thoughtful rather than expensive, made such a warm impression on her that she recommended that same hotel to her close friend Noel Coward."

Caring enough to remember puts you on a special footing with people that is deep, lasting, and ultimately, the most satisfying aspect of your career.

Lesson 5

You Have To Give A Piece Of Your Mind To Get Peace of Mind.

All my life I've hated losing track of people. One of the best things about writing a book was hearing from people I hadn't heard from since I was a kid. I even heard from people who knew my parents but who I'd never met. I remember a very old gentleman in a nursing home who wrote to tell me he had known my father back in the 1930s. He described the kind of man my father had been and said how happy he was to make my acquaintance after all these years.

People like him are irreplaceable. That's why it's so important to have a way to keep track of them. The 80/20 rule is never more true than it is with the Rolodex file. You probably will be actively in touch with only twenty percent of the people listed in your Rolodex at any given time. For your most important contacts, you need *quality* information that is current, correct and readily accessible.

For the other eighty percent, you need a system that can handle *quantity*. In other words, you want to be able to stay up to date with a large number of people without a lot of cumbersome paperwork or a confusing system that will make you want to avoid the matter entirely. You want to know that the eighty percent are there to fall back on and to call on when you need them.

Years ago I made an acquisition of another envelope company. The company was left in trust with seven trustees. Everybody and their brother was trying to buy it. It was no secret. They let the whole industry know that the company was for sale. However, seven people had to make the final decision. I went immediately to the old Rolodex file and started to network to see who knew any of those trustees. Could I ask them to make calls to testify in favor of my integrity and character, and to let the trustees know that I would be good for the company?

Over a long period of time, I was successful. I did make the acquisition, and I believe that my Rolodex was the leg up, the cutting edge, that paved the way. When the vote was taken, I knew I had people in the room who were on my side because I had taken the trouble to learn who the decision makers were, and had asked people to contact them on my behalf. I had also learned that one of the trustees' biggest concerns was that after the company was sold it would be merged to eliminate it as a competitor and people would lose their jobs. Through my network, I was able to reassure the trustees that my word was good and the company would remain intact.

I've heard it said of one of my mentors that he can "see around corners." I think that ability to see beyond your own line of vision is the greatest gift the Rolodex file can give. Almost all of our knowledge and insight comes from other people.

I often hear people repeating the old line that you never know where your next great idea is going to come from. I don't believe it. I know exactly where it is. It's somewhere buried in my Rolodex file, just waiting for me to find it.

Lesson 6

Make It Work For You,
Not Against You.

If the Rolodex file isn't working at least as hard as you are, there's something wrong. The same systems don't work for everyone. I certainly learned that with writing. Some people can sit in front of an intimidating, space age computer that cost more than my house and type away without batting an eye.

I, on the other hand, still find myself hunched over a yellow legal pad, pen in hand, scratching out an illegible scrawl that very few people in the world are able to translate. It's not a pretty style. But it works for me.[2]

That's how you need to manage your Rolodex file. Once your system's in place, analyze it. See what works and what doesn't. Identify the parts that are easy, or even fun. Those are the keepers. Then think about the parts you can't stand. If

[2]In 1993 a new company I started in Atlanta called Cogni Tech launched Sharkware, a contact and activity management system that is turning my Rolodex into a computerized wonder. Write to me for information on this Windows application.

you're not doing something after thirty days, you certainly won't do it for the next thirty years. And that doesn't mean you've failed Rolodex 101, it just means a change in plan.

If I had to name the single characteristic shared by all the truly successful people I've met in my lifetime, I'd have to say it's the ability to create and nurture a network of contacts. But everyone does it differently.

Jeana Yeager and Dick Rutan designed the experimental airplane, Voyager, and flew it on a historic nonstop flight around the world in 1986. They became experts at grassroots networking during the years they were trying to put together enough money to build the plane. In their book, *Voyager: One Flight, One World*, they recount that they were initially extremely naïve about fundraising. Soon, however, they realized that the last thing a corporate sponsor wanted to do was put its name on something that was likely to end up a glowing fireball on the evening news.

The team decided that individual donors might want to contribute to a project that was being done privately, the "American do-it-yourself way." Jeana came up with the idea of forming a "Voyager Impressive People Club" (the VIPs), with each member contributing $100. "The VIPs became not only financial boosters, but personal ones, calling to find out how things were going, bringing their friends by. We couldn't have made it without them."

The VIPs were soon joined by countless people who couldn't afford the $100 but had heard about the project and wanted to help. One letter, which the design team framed and hung on the wall of the hangar, contained two one-dollar bills. "Don't laugh," it said, "I don't get lunch today."

Only you know what approach to network building works best for you. Here are some suggestions:

One young consultant has an ironclad rule that he doesn't leave his office in the evening until he's organized whatever needs to be entered into the Rolodex by his secretary the next day. Another friend throws everything he collects for the week into a shoe box near the front door, then empties and sorts it out first thing Monday morning.

A longtime vendor to Mackay Envelope has another system. She pulls the cards of all the people she intends to contact during the upcoming week and places them in little piles on her desk. One pile is for those she wants to visit and another is for those she will telephone. A third pile goes to her secretary who prepares envelopes so that when she has a spare minute during the week she can send handwritten notes.

THE ROLODEX NETWORK BUILDER

Lately, I've gone through all the cards and had my assistants create a smaller Rolodex card file that contains just birthdays. That way I can roll through it to the upcoming month and make sure I send a card or make a birthday phone call. I've also made a copy of my Rolodex file so I can keep one at the office and an identical one at home. When my secretaries make a new card, they make two of them—one for each place. The only tricky part of this system is getting me to take them home and file them. Sometimes my memory is the thing I forget with!

The latest studies done on creativity show that the use of color is a huge factor in both learning and retention. I've applied that idea to my Rolodex file. There are a couple ways to do it. One is to color code groups of Rolodex file cards you want to separate by function. Customers are alphabetized behind the red divider, prospects are alphabetized behind the green, personal friends and relatives are blue, etc. You can do this with either color cards or plastic card protectors manufactured by Rolodex.

Another method that's proved helpful is entering handwritten notes on the cards in a different color each year. That way, if I've talked to a friend and updated his or her card with this year's color, I can tell at a glance we've been in contact recently and I have new information. This is particularly handy for those quick shuffles through the cards for people I've talked to lately and with whom I've been out of touch.

It doesn't matter how crazy or outlandish your system becomes. As long as it fulfills two criteria: it's fun, and it works.

Make Connections
The Old-Fashioned Way.

John D. Rockefeller once said of interpersonal skills: "I'd pay more for that ability than for any other under the sun." My father, Jack B. Mackay, possessed a greater gift than anyone else I've ever known for getting along with people.

Jack Mackay was the local Associated Press reporter in the days before car phones, fax machines and computers. The only way he could possibly get the information he needed was to know enough people who would share it with him. As a kid, I was amazed that whenever we walked down the street he could hardly take ten steps without someone calling out, "Hi, Jack!" I also remember his dog-eared Rolodex file in its prominent place next to the teletype machine. I don't know how he could even read it, but he did, and his career depended on it.

As I was growing up, when I asked my father a question, he didn't always know the answer, but he always knew someone who did. That's a great lesson for a child to learn. You don't have to know everything, as long as you know people who know the things you don't.

In my opinion, one of the greatest mistakes you can make when you're just starting your career is being afraid to ask for help. Most so-called "gurus" are downright flattered when someone asks their opinion, on anything—whether they know something about it or not. People love to share their knowledge and opinions. If you've ever been at a cocktail party and happened to mention teenagers, or travel or golf, or dog training, you'll understand what I mean. One of my favorite charities just scored a coup by acquiring, at no charge, the services of a highly paid marketing consultant. When asked why she chose to work with that particular group, she replied, "You were the first ones to ask."

I've used my Rolodex file to make connections for friends, friends of friends, employees, and customers. My kids have benefited, too. When my daughter, Mimi, spent her junior year abroad in Madrid, I wandered through my Rolodex and found a treasure trove of names of people she could contact. What might have been a siesta year became a fiesta year!

Any type of contact can ultimately contribute toward your long term goals. I received an unexpected invitation to speak to the international sales force of a major corporation. After a little digging, I learned that they had invited me because my speech coach sat next to their special events coordinator one Sunday in church.

When you're making connections with people, they aren't always the most obvious ones. That's why I use a specialized format for organizing information. If all I wrote down was name, address, phone number and place of business, I'd be limited to those kinds of connections. But I like to keep track of the special things—the extra things people do with their lives.

If you were job hunting and asked me for the name of someone in advertising, for example, I could probably respond off the top of my head (on a good day). But if I use my Rolodex file, I can tell you the name of an advertising person who loves tennis like you do, belongs to the same political party, lives in your neighborhood, has a child at your alma mater, comes from your small town...you get the picture.

When I first decided to write a book, my writing experience was limited to a few articles in regional magazines. I had a lot of ideas, but didn't have a clue how to organize them into a readable format, let alone how to find anyone to publish them. That was one occasion where my Rolodex file proved invaluable.

After a little searching, I realized I had a number of contacts who could provide me with the help I needed. They weren't necessarily the first people who might spring to mind—authors and the like—but they were people who could help. Without my Rolodex file, I never would have thought of them.

One of them was the proverbial "high school nerd turned success" story. In the years since high school, I've tracked the careers of a lot of people I assumed I might never see again, but in whom I had some spark of interest. One of them was a fellow I'll call Dale. He was your quintessential introvert, perennially on the outside of whatever the popular kids were doing, probably off in his own little world thinking about how he was eventually going to succeed if he survived adolescence. I always liked him, and, even though we didn't have a lot in common, I always made a point of speaking with him when I saw him.

Since graduation, I had probably seen him only four or five times, but we kept in occasional contact through Christmas cards, and I enjoyed sending and receiving a brief update.

Thirty-five years later, I found myself in the shoes of the first-time author trying to ensure that my book was going to make it. Digging through my Rolodex file, I spotted a familiar name. It was Dale, and I noted that he had gone into something related to the book business. I tracked him down, and it turned out that he had become one of the largest wholesale book distributors on the West Coast. I contacted him and he placed an order for 10,000 books, ten times the usual order. When I thanked him he said, "I have always remembered our friendship in high school. It's meant a lot to me."

Lesson 8

Unlock The Secrets
Of The Universe.

It may sound like I'm exaggerating, but most of the important secrets of the universe can be found in my Rolodex file. Granted, the pyramids don't quite fit, and I never have understood the theory of relativity. But a lot of the *other* important secrets are there. Like who gives money to what favorite charity, or who used to work for whom.

You say those don't sound like very exciting secrets? Well, the theory of relativity isn't so exciting either if you don't know how to use it.

There's a man named Barnett Lipton who has made himself both rich and famous by producing spectacles. Not the kind you wear, but the kind you watch. He produced the opening ceremonies at the 1984 Olympics in Los Angeles (Remember the 84 pianos?) and has gone on to do the half-time shows for several Super Bowls among other things.

When asked what he had in mind for the opening ceremonies at the 1990 U.S. Olympic Festival, Lipton said the audience could expect at least "five wows"—five unforgettable special effects.

I'm crazy about that concept of *wowing* the audience, whatever the occasion. If you and I could make a sales call or a job interview as exciting as an opening ceremony, we'd win every time. All we need are the "wows," and we probably don't even need five of them.

Lipton competes in a class by himself where every production contains more wows than the last one. Fortunately for us—and unfortunately for our customers—we don't. The last time your customer, or the person sitting across the desk from you in a job interview, experienced something that made them sit up and say "wow" was probably long ago, if it's ever happened at all.

How do we go from humdrum to "wow?" The answer is simple even though most people will never think of it. It's in the Rolodex file.

Barnett Lipton knows the only way to create a fantastic half-time show for the Super Bowl or an Olympic opening ceremony is to know his customer, which in this case is the audience. He knows what they *expect* and he knows what they *don't expect*—and he fulfills both. That's exactly the same mission we have in selling.

First, we have to know what the audience *expects*. For a half-time spectacle, it's a zillion bands, a zillion dancers on platforms and a laser light show. For a sales call, it's being on time, well-prepared and knowledgeable about your product, with a sense of humor thrown in.

Second, and this is the part most people ignore, we have to know what the audience *doesn't expect*. Because it's the unexpected that makes us unforgettable.

What the customer doesn't expect is that you'll go the extra mile to make an impression. They don't expect that you'll know about their recent problems with on-time delivery, or that they've added a subsidiary in Tuscaloosa. They certainly don't expect that you've done your homework on how your company could participate in their new company-wide quality assurance program.

When I was writing my second book, *Beware The Naked Man Who Offers You His Shirt*, I was asked to appear on the Oprah Winfrey Show. One of the main ideas I wanted to get across was how important it is to really know your customer. As a guest, I knew what was expected of me because I'd watched probably a hundred other authors hit the interview circuit and perform the same old tricks. I decided to do the unexpected.

First, I hightailed it to the library and did a computer search on everything written about Oprah over the last several years. Then I made copious notes and tucked them into my briefcase.

THE ROLODEX NETWORK BUILDER

Imagine her surprise on network television when I reached down under my chair, pulled out a four-foot long computer printout and proclaimed, "Before we talk about me, Oprah, let's talk about you!"

It was all there. Her childhood, family, education, early career, later successes. She'd been on 62 magazine covers and I could name all of them. It brought the show to a standstill.

These unexpected but welcome "wows" don't come from out of the blue. They come out of your Rolodex file.

All my life I've been a voracious, if unpredictable, reader. I'll read whatever I can get my hands on—especially if it pertains to my business or my customers. As I read, I highlight points of interest and clip out pertinent items. Usually, the greatest ideas are the simplest. I'm looking for the little gem of information that makes me stop and say "wow." And when that gem applies to a customer, a prospect, an associate or a friend—you guessed it, it goes in the Rolodex file. You don't have to write a lot, just a little note to remind you of your big idea. That's where the "wows" come from.

Lesson 9

You Can Improve on Human Nature.

An ancient Chinese proverb advises:

> *If you want one year of prosperity, grow grain.*
> *If you want ten years of prosperity, grow trees.*
> *If you want one hundred years of prosperity, grow people.*

Deep down, we all know it's true, yet fear very often keeps us from maximizing our contacts with other people. Fear is a real key. Human beings are full of fears; we procrastinate, we don't trust ourselves, we're afraid that we'll fail.

One of the most brilliant individuals I know, an inventor of medical products, has an office that looks like it was touched by Hurricane Hugo. Papers cover the desks, the tables, the walls and the floor. He even has things taped to the lampshades! When I asked him why he let it get this way he answered, "I'm afraid if I put all this away, I won't be able to find anything!"

In our company, my office is notorious as a sort of organizational Bermuda Triangle. Many things go in, but unless my assistants attack with shovels, nothing ever comes out. That's because

THE ROLODEX NETWORK BUILDER

I've always been an information junkie. I just can't pass up an intriguing business book, a good article, the latest audio cassette tape, or anything else that might strike my fancy.

The single exception, the method to my madness, has always been the Rolodex card file. For me, it's more than a habit. It's a way of life. If I can keep track of the people and affiliations that are important to me, then I know the rest of the business will fall into place.

The key, of course, is discipline. Whenever I share my philosophies about organizing and using the Rolodex, I get flack from my sales force. "Why give it away?" they groan. "We've worked so hard, let's keep it to ourselves." My response is always the same. Number one, no matter how well anybody else uses it, we've got a thirty-year head start on them. Number two, ninety percent of the people that hear about it will never put it into practice away.

In my entire career I have never once heard a successful person say he regretted putting time and energy into keeping his Rolodex. It's one of the few tools that's absolutely, positively guaranteed to work. Experts on human behavior say that it takes just thirty days of consistent practice to form a new habit. It's amazing to me that so few people are willing to persist in something for

46

thirty days, especially considering the rewards.

Once I had to hire an attorney to negotiate a property deal for me and several limited partners in New York. Anyone who knows anything about New York real estate deals knows that it is a contact business—building inspectors, drain commissioners, construction union bosses, and an endless list of go-betweens.

I insisted that the last two interviews be held in the finalists' own offices. Did I look at their hunting trophies or the oriental rugs on their floors? Was I impressed by how many pictures of handshakes with borough presidents bedecked the walls, or the script on the Juris Doctor degree? No, I looked to see how big and how dog-eared their respective Rolodex files were.

The desk of the first attorney boasted a mammoth Rolodex file that looked like it had been chewed by a pack of wild animals. The second attorney's desk displayed only a neat leather address book. I checked his secretary's desk. No Rolodex file there, either. As attorney number two leaned back in his chair, I noticed he was wearing the finest looking watch I'd ever seen. Rolex or Rolodex? Which one do you think I chose?

One of the greatest human fears is of asking for what we really want. If we're not very good at asking it, we'll feel foolish and fear we might get turned down. Yet, if we make a science of it, we're afraid of being seen as manipulative.

It all comes down to liking people. I get a real kick out of adding people to my Rolodex file. I might not see someone for five or ten years, but sooner or later they crop up again, and it's always fun to get reacquainted.

One of my favorite quotes on the subject comes from Conrad Hilton. He wrote of his early success, "I do believe in luck. But the kind I believe in has to do with people...The value of buddies was something you learned in the Army where your life depended on how well a hundred other men carried out their assignments. In the Army you were as good as your buddies...Later, when I reached the rarefied air of Big Business, I learned to call them 'associates.' The facts remained the same. All my life I have only been as good as my associates, and in them have found my good luck, my fortune."

Lesson 10

Never Say No For The Other Guy.

Every three or four months I give myself a treat. I take a few hours out of the day, shut the door, sit at my desk and just roll all over the world through my Rolodex file. I'll call Istanbul or Indianapolis or wherever strikes my fancy just to say, "Hello, how are you," and it's terrific, especially when I contact people I haven't talked to for a while.

Since my children have gotten old enough to grab a backpack and take off on their own pilgrimages, it's been great fun to watch them get in touch with old friends who live in places slightly more exotic than Minneapolis/St. Paul. I would have been far more worried about some of their travels if they hadn't known they had lists of names and numbers of people to call in every city along the way—all gleaned from the Rolodex file.

I decided to cross-reference my Rolodex file by city. That way, if I know I'm going to Orlando, for example, I can pull the names of all the people who live there and decide who to look up when I arrive.

As a lifelong tennis enthusiast, one of my greatest fantasies was to some day find myself sitting in a center court box at Wimbledon. Now, for those of you who are as ignorant about the intricacies of such things as I was, I will tell you that you and I have about as much chance of getting courtside seats at Wimbledon as you do in arranging to borrow the crown jewels. In fact, it may even be harder, since I know who has the crown jewels, but I didn't have a clue who was in possession of those great seats that are mysteriously handed down from generation to generation.

Like most people, I hate revealing my ignorance. But each time I do it, I remind myself that the worst thing I'm going to hear is "no," and even if I hear a "no," I'm going to learn something.

I decided to ask an old friend who had become a banker in London. I figured I had nothing to lose except the long distance charges for the time it took him to quit laughing, so I found his number in my Rolodex and gave him a call.

After the usual pleasantries and a little hedging, I popped the question. Imagine my surprise when, instead of laughter, I heard silence. Then I heard the magic word, "Maybe we can work something out." It seems his bank was one of the oldest banks in London and had, since time immemorial, held a small block of priceless Wimbledon tickets that it parceled out to "favored" clients.

Lately, the bank's fortunes had declined slightly and they had begun looking for ways to add some influential American companies to their corporate client base. Introductions to those companies might be worth more to the bank's bottom line than the good will they engendered each year handing out tickets to existing customers.

The end of the story shouldn't seem so surprising, but it still amazes me. A search through my Rolodex provided me with names of friends who I thought might have an interest in banking with a London bank, and several months later, there I sat in my version of the crown jewels—courtside seats at the greatest tennis tournament in the world!

In May, 1990, history was made in my home state. When Soviet Premier Mikhail Gorbachev first announced plans to visit the United States, everyone assumed he would visit the old standby, Washington, D.C.

Rudy Perpich, the Governor of Minnesota, hatched the crazy notion that Gorbachev might also like to visit some other parts of the country. So he wrote him a letter. And he asked seventy

Russian students on campus at the University of Minnesota to write him letters as well telling him how great it would be for him to see the Heartland.

Perpich asked for the order, risked that he would be turned down, and to everyone's amazement, he got what he wanted. For a day in June, Minnesota turned itself upside down to welcome one of the most influential leaders in modern history!

The moral? Never say no for the other guy. Most people avoid risks their whole life by assuming the other guy is going to say no. You have your whole Rolodex with all its awesome power right in front of you. All you have to do is ask. I guarantee you, if you get enough no's, you're bound to get a few yesses. So don't say no for anyone. You never know when you'll create for yourself the opportunity of a lifetime.

Conclusion

When good things happen to me, I'm often tempted to believe there's something magical about them...and maybe there is. But, I'm not about to sit back passively and wait for the magic to kick in. I want to give it every possible opportunity to happen.

For years I had a plaque on the wall that read as follows: "Pray for a good harvest...but keep on hoeing!"

I looked at that so many times over the years that it's permanently burned into my memory.

If you want your Rolodex file to produce a fruitful harvest, you have to be persistent and you have to keep on hoeing. Remember:

1. **It's A Chronicle of Your Life.** As the world changes, one thing will remain constant—the relationships you develop over a lifetime.

2. **Guard It With Your Life.** Don't forget the most important word in the English language. It's Rolodex®.

3. **Consider It An Investment.** We all start out in life with the same amount of time. It's what we do with it that counts.

4. **Remembering Doesn't Work.** He who

counts on his memory has a fool for a filing system.

5. **You Have To Give A Piece of Your Mind To Get Peace of Mind.** You can utilize the insight and vision of your whole network to help you "see around corners."

6. **Make It Work For You, Not Against You.** With your Rolodex file, only two things count: it's fun, and it works.

7. **Make Connections The Old-Fashioned Way.** You don't have to know everything. Seek out people who know the things you don't.

8. **Unlock The Secrets of The Universe.** Give them what they expect, then "wow" them with the unexpected.

9. **You Can Improve On Human Nature.** With practice, using your Rolodex file becomes more than a discipline, it's a way of life.

10. **Never Say No for The Other Guy.** Your next great opportunity is there, somewhere, buried in your Rolodex file, just waiting for you to find it.

The greatest joy of my Rolodex file is knowing I can make the world a smaller, friendlier place by reaching out to the network of people I've gotten to know over the years. It has changed my life…and I guarantee it will change yours.

End

Appendix I

Self-Test:
How Good Are Your
Network Building Skills?

**Answer these questions and rate yourself on a
1-5 scale, *1* being not true and 5 being very true:**

1. I have a large network of people I
   can call upon when I need help,
   information, or a resource. ① 2 3 4 5

2. When I meet someone new, I record
   and file information about that
   person within 24 hours. ① 2 3 4 5

3. I add somebody new to my Rolodex
   file at least every week. ① 2 3 4 5

4. I follow up with new contacts right
   away—writing a note, making a
   phone call, or sending a clipping. ① 2 3 4 5

55

5. I keep track of special things that matter to my contacts like their family, hobbies and achievements.

   ① 2 3 4 5

6. I can easily find out when I was last in contact with someone.

   ① 2 3 4 5

7. When I mail something out—a resume, sales letter, change of address—I can count on having correct name spellings, titles, addresses for everyone in my network.

   ① 2 3 4 5

8. I know about and acknowledge special dates like birthdays, anniversaries and graduations.

   1 ② 3 4 5

9. When I want to give a business gift, I can count on my Rolodex file to provide me with an excellent idea of what the person might like.

   ① 2 3 4 5

10. I make it easy for others to add me to their network by providing my business card, notifying them of address changes, and informing them about my career progress.

    ① 2 3 4 5

11. When friends ask me for the name of a good resource, I have no trouble providing one. ① 2 3 4 5

12. When the moment comes, I can really "wow" a customer, prospect or potential employer with special information or an idea that shows I care. 1 2 3 4 5

Total the points above and score yourself:

0-24   You're in rough shape. It's time to make a change.

25-36   You're doing some things right. Now let's get to work.

37-44   You're off to a great start. Build on what you've done so far.

45-55   You've got superstar potential. All you need is the polish.

56-60   You're already there. Keep up the great effort!

Appendix II

Network Builder Cards
(Front)

```
Name _____
Phone  H _____  W _____
Title _____
Company _____
Address _____
Birthdate & Place _____
Connections _____
          _____
Family _____
```

1.   **Name.** This one is obvious, but you should include any nicknames or casual forms of address that you or your office staff will use in correspondence.

2.   **Title.** Keep this up to date for use in correspondence, and it's a good idea to acknowledge promotions and job changes as soon as you hear of them.

3.   **Company.** I'm amazed at how many letters I receive that have my name and/or my company's name spelled incorrectly. Being sloppy

about such personal details is the best way to ruin a first impression.

4. **Address.** Keep your Rolodex Network Builder up to date with any address changes. Sending a short "Congratulations on your new office!" note is a great way to keep in touch, and sends the message that you are well-organized.

5. **Birthdate and Place.** I'm a stickler for keeping track of birthdays, and I like to know where people were born because it tells me a lot about them. One of the most successful people I know always seemed unapproachable until I found out he came from a tiny town of 800 people on the Iron Range in Minnesota, near the town where my mother was born.

6. **Connections.** This is the place to jog your memory as to where you met someone, who introduced you, what activity you shared, and when you last saw one another. As the years go by, these old connections can be invaluable.

7. **Family.** Family information about people in your network is important for *you* to know because it's so important to *them*. I include items about spouses and children, as well as their activities, whenever possible.

(Back)

Education	
Affiliations	
Special Interests	
Significant Career History	
Accomplishments	
Wow	

8. **Education.** Educational background is something many people feel strongly about. As National President of the University of Minnesota Alumni Association, I was constantly amazed by the level of commitment and enthusiasm exhibited by alumni members. Even decades after graduation, they continued to feel intensely connected to the place where they began their adult lives.

9. **Affiliations.** This includes memberships in professional organizations, churches, clubs, political groups, etc. I've met people all over the world and developed some wonderful friendships based simply on our mutual membership in an organization. It's a great conversation starter and gives otherwise busy people a good excuse to stay in touch.

10. **Special Interests.** Here I try to record what Joseph Campbell refers to as a person's "bliss"—that is whatever, besides work, makes a

person really light up. I recently discovered that one of my old friends is fascinated with space exploration and I sent him some clippings about the Hubble Telescope. You would have thought I'd sent him a million dollars.

11. **Significant Career History.** This includes brief notes on anything you want to remember about someone's career, such as a big promotion, a lay-off in his or her company, or the name of a former employer.

12. **Accomplishments.** I love keeping track of awards, publications, promotions and achievements of people I care about because I know how much effort went into them.

13. **Wow.** This is a space I leave for recording any tidbit of information that could make our next meeting unforgettable. Little things mean so much to most people. On a recent trip to Stockholm, I picked up that day's newspaper (in Swedish, of course) for a transplanted Swedish friend living in Minneapolis. He usually waits two weeks for papers to arrive in the local library and reads them there. Imagine his delight at receiving, unexpectedly, fresh news from home the same day it was printed.

Harvey Mackay Rolodex Network Builder cards are available by writing to me at 2100 Elm Street S.E. Minneapolis, MN 55414 and enclosing $2.00 for each package of 100 cards.

Appendix III

Cross-Section:
Typical Rolodex® Card File

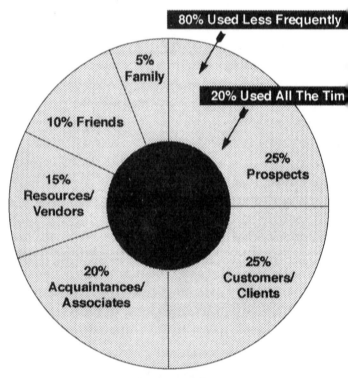

80% Used Less Frequently

20% Used All The Tim

5% Family

10% Friends

15% Resources/ Vendors

20% Acquaintances/ Associates

25% Prospects

25% Customers/ Clients

Total = 100%